E*x*p*ect**a**t**i*ONS
Not So Great

*A Relationship Exercise
For All Couples In Love*

Richard Fruncillo MD PhD

Copyright © 2012 Richard Fruncillo M.D. Ph.D.
All rights reserved.

ISBN: 1468000934
ISBN 13: 9781468000931

Part A

Directions

This book consists of two identical parts labeled Part A and Part B.

Ideally, both partners should complete this exercise at the same time. It should take about an hour or so to answer the questions, and then both partners should review their answers with each other and have a discussion.

To begin, you must rip the book in half. Find the middle of the book where Part B begins, fold the book back and forth several times vertically so that there is a significant crease in the side binding of the book, and then gently rip the book into two parts. You will not need to use anything but your fingers. Each partner then takes a book part and begins the exercise, and hopefully, you will be on your way to a **win-win** relationship.

Introduction

I am not a psychologist, psychiatrist or relationship expert. I am a physician and a scientist who has spent almost forty years as an adult watching the same roller-coaster pattern of relationship deterioration over and over again. It goes something like this:

1. You see someone that you are attracted to.
2. You meet them.
3. You date.
4. The neurotransmitters in your brain trigger so much pleasure that attention and critical thinking are impaired.
5. You can't get enough of the other person.
6. You decide to get married or live together, thinking that the "happy" neurotransmitters will stimulate your brain for the rest of your life.
7. Everyday issues lead to minor conflicts.
8. Your partner reacts to these conflicts in an unanticipated and sometimes confrontational way.
9. You become confused and don't understand this behavior.
10. Time goes by and these negative encounters become more frequent.
11. You convince yourself that your partner has changed.
12. As more time passes, you lose all sense of happiness with the relationship.
13. You avoid communication as a defense measure.
14. The relationship remains at this low level or ends.

INTRODUCTION

Sound familiar? What happened? I believe a major part of the answer lies with **expectations**. When a relationship is flying high, we engage in subconscious (and sometimes conscious) assumptions about our partner to avoid the interruption of the "feel good" neurotransmitters. We conclude, "If my partner loves me, he or she must agree with everything about me, including my quirky habits, beliefs, ethics, and everyday behaviors." So when we are finally confronted with the reality that we differ from our partner over an issue, we become disappointed because our **expectations** have been shattered. Thus begins the negative tailspin.

What can you do? You could see a relationship counselor, but I believe a more logical approach, consistent with modern trends in twenty-first century medicine, is one of prevention. If couples understand early in the relationship how their partners think about numerous everyday issues that could arise in the future, then the negative energy and feelings from broken **expectations** could be minimized, and replaced with the positive energy of **compromise**. When a conflicting issue surfaces, if you already know what your partner's reaction is going to be, you can offer a **compromise** instead of an argument.

When you think about it, we spend the entire day resolving minor conflicts in our personal lives by making **compromise** decisions. *Should I buy this or save the money? Should I wear a tie or be more comfortable without?* Since we know all about us, it is easy to make a balanced **compromise** decision that maximizes the positive and minimizes the negative aspects of our choice. This is a **win-win** decision— the gold standard for conflict resolution. Your goal is to have **win-win** relationship interactions in which you and your partner feel good about the result, and the positive energy keeps flowing.

NOT SO GREAT EXPECTATIONS

This book consists of a series of questions relating to common issues that come up in the course of two people being together in a committed relationship. They are grouped into categories in no special order. Obviously, not all questions will be relevant to any one relationship, but you should answer most. It is my hope that this book will be a significant catalyst for a "couple discovery" process. After dividing the book into its two identical parts, both partners should answer all of the questions alone.

After completion, the couple should come together and go over the questions one by one. Hopefully this will lead to some meaningful relationship insight, some resolution of controversial issues, and some good, old-fashioned fun.

I must caution you that this question book has never been formally tested, and there is the possibility of a negative outcome for some couples, so proceed at your own risk. If you have significant problems compromising, you should consider: 1) Bringing the results of this exercise to a couples' counselor, or 2) Reading other books on compromising skills. I think that the majority of couples will have more positive than negative results from the exercise as long as you set aside your **expectations**, think **compromise**, and aim for **win-win** outcomes.

Topics

Children	1
Money	4
Employment	7
Relatives	10
Food/Cooking	12
Sleep	14
Past Relationships	17
Pets	20
Vacations	23
Holidays	27
Hobbies	29
Religion	31
School/Education	34
Health	36
Sports	38
House/Home Life	40
Marriage Ceremony	44
Appearance	46
Shopping	47
Addictions	48
Intimacy	50
Politics	52
Time	53
Friends	54
Miscellaneous	56

Disclaimer

This book is for entertainment purposes only. It is not meant to provide relationship counseling, and it cannot diagnose and treat any psychological condition or disease. Neither the author nor the publisher can be responsible for any damages that are perceived to result from the use of this book.

Children

How many children do you want to have? ___

If you couldn't have children, would you consider:
    Adoption? ☐ Yes ☐ Not sure ☐ No
    In-vitro fertilization? ☐ Yes ☐ Not sure ☐ No
    Surrogate mother? ☐ Yes ☐ Not sure ☐ No
    Sperm bank? ☐ Yes ☐ Not sure ☐ No

Would you keep having children to have one of the opposite sex?
    ☐ Yes   ☐ Not sure   ☐ No

At what age would you like to start having children? ___

At what age would you like to stop having children? ___

If you had an ectopic pregnancy, would you want to continue to have children?
    ☐ Yes   ☐ Not sure   ☐ No

If you were told you were going to have a child with Down Syndrome, would you keep the child?
    ☐ Yes   ☐ Not sure   ☐ No

If you had a seriously autistic child, would you consider placing the child in an institution?
    ☐ Yes   ☐ Not sure   ☐ No

What kind of school do you prefer that your children attend?
- ☐ Public school
- ☐ Private school
- ☐ Private religious school
- ☐ Home school

Do you believe in spanking children?
- ☐ Yes, that's how I was raised
- ☐ Sometimes, in extreme circumstances
- ☐ Never

How would you feel about your children trying out for contact sports?
- ☐ Whatever they would want to do is fine
- ☐ Yes, but not football or hockey
- ☐ No contact sports

At what age would you allow your child to sleep over a friend's house?
- ☐ 4–5
- ☐ 6–7
- ☐ 8–9
- ☐ 10–11
- ☐ 12–13
- ☐ Never

Whom would you allow to babysit your child?
- ☐ Close family and friends
- ☐ Referred adults and teenagers
- ☐ Only referred adults
- ☐ Nobody

Which of the following best describes your attitude toward having adult children living with you in your home?
- ☐ They can stay as long as they want.
- ☐ They can stay for a year or two, until they save enough money for a place of their own.

- ☐ They are adults, and they need to make whatever sacrifices it takes to live on their own; allowing them to live with me would do more harm than good.

If you and your partner will be traveling on a plane without your children, do you believe in taking separate planes?

☐ Yes ☐ Not sure ☐ No

Would it bother you if your partner insisted on naming your child after themselves or their parents?

☐ Yes ☐ Not sure ☐ No

Would you ever want to enter your young child in a pageant or talent contest?

☐ Yes ☐ Not sure ☐ No

How would you react if your child told you that they were going to enlist in the military?

- ☐ I support it. It is a very honorable thing to do.
- ☐ I do not support it, but I will not stop it.
- ☐ I will do everything possible to discourage it.

Would you want to send your children to a camp for part of the summer?

☐ Yes ☐ Not sure ☐ No

Would you ever want to send your children to stay with relatives for part of the summer?

☐ Yes ☐ Not sure ☐ No

✲ ✲ ✲

Money

Who will manage the money in the household?
 ☐ Myself   ☐ My partner   ☐ Both of us

What type of banking arrangement do you envision?
 ☐ One account: everything comes from it
 ☐ Separate accounts: one partner pays for certain things, and the other partner pays for other things
 ☐ Three accounts: one for all household expenses, and separate personal accounts for each partner
 ☐ Other

In order of importance, rank your five top priorities for spending money:
 __Home __Home furnishings __Vacations
 __Personal education
 __Entertainment (movies, cable, sports, shows)
 __Children's education   __Nice cars
 __Drinking/drugs   __Gambling
 __Investments __Restaurants
 __Retirement savings __Children's college savings
 __New clothing __Jewelry __Gifts to family
 __Child expenses (clothes, toys, classes, parties, etc.)
 _____Other

How much of your combined income would you like to donate to charity?
 ☐ None   ☐ About 1%   ☐ 1–3%
 ☐ 3–5%   ☐ Greater than 5%

MONEY

If one of us works and the other manages the home, how will we make decisions regarding money?
- ☐ The working person will be the decision maker, and the other partner will need permission to spend money.
- ☐ The working person will pay all the bills and allow the other a monthly allowance of money for personal spending.
- ☐ Both partners will always have a say in how we spend money.
- ☐ Other

How much credit card debt is too much?
- ☐ Over $1,000 ☐ Over $5,000 ☐ Over $10,000
- ☐ Over $20,000

Would you ever consider bankruptcy?
- ☐ Yes ☐ Not sure ☐ No

If you found out that your partner took out a credit card without your knowledge and owed over $5,000 on it, how would you react?
- ☐ I expect them to pay it off as soon as possible.
- ☐ I am upset about the secrecy.
- ☐ It could end the relationship.

How do you feel about spending money on children?
- ☐ My children will have whatever they want.
- ☐ My children will get presents on birthdays/holidays, and a weekly allowance.
- ☐ My children will get presents on birthdays/holidays, and a weekly allowance in exchange for doing chores.
- ☐ My children will get some presents, but they will be expected to help around the house for no allowance.

Which of the following best describes your attitude toward spending money?
- ☐ Pay for everything in cash except your house and car, and avoid debt at all costs.
- ☐ It is normal and acceptable to have some credit card debt.
- ☐ You are only young once and could be dead tomorrow, so don't deny yourself anything that can be bought on credit.

Which of the following best describes your attitude toward investing money?
- ☐ I want my money either in low risk CDs or at home in my mattress.
- ☐ I would like the customary level of investment risk for my age.
- ☐ I believe in a high-risk, high reward strategy. You can't get rich by leaving your money in the bank.

Would you ever want to invest in real estate and become a landlord?
☐ Yes   ☐ Not sure   ☐ No

Do you like to invest in common stocks that you pick yourself?
☐ Yes   ☐ Sometimes   ☐ No

✫ ✫ ✫

Employment

Would you consider a job opportunity that involved significant (greater than 50 % of the time) long- distance travel?
 ☐ Yes   ☐ Not sure   ☐ No

If you were happy in a location and your children were in the local school system, would you consider moving to another state so that either you or your partner could have a better employment opportunity?
 ☐ Yes   ☐ Not sure   ☐ No

How would you feel if your partner was considering a promotion that involved a 40% raise but required a 50–60 hour work week with weekend work?
- ☐ I welcome it and will modify our lifestyle accordingly.
- ☐ I don't like it, but I am willing to give it a try for a year or two to see if we can adapt.
- ☐ I am against it. Family time and lack of stress are more important than the extra money.

If your partner was the primary income producer and lost his or her job, would you be willing to work extra—or even two jobs—until he or she found another job in their field?
- ☐ Yes.
- ☐ Yes, but after a while I would expect them to find some type of job to help out.

☐ No, my partner should take any job he could find while looking for a job in his area. I should not be expected to work more.

Imagine that your partner is the primary income producer and has a good job and benefits. If he or she suddenly decided to leave his or her employment and start his or her own company, knowing the risks and financial struggles, how would you react?
☐ I completely support him or her. Owning one's own business is the American dream.
☐ I will only support it if the sacrifice is not too great, and I will only give it a limited period of time to work out.
☐ I am against it, as the risk is too great. In these times, you should be happy you have a good job with good benefits.

In a family with young children, do you consider it important for one of the parents to not work and stay at home?
☐ Yes   ☐ Not sure   ☐ No

Which of the following best describes your philosophy?
☐ Work hard, invest in the future
☐ Work hard, play hard
☐ Work enough to get by; time for family and friends is most important
☐ You are only young once; do whatever you have to do to get by, and work only when you have to

Would you allow your partner to take a job that involved working predominately with members of the opposite sex?
☐ Yes   ☐ Not sure   ☐ No

EMPLOYMENT

Would you allow your partner to take a job that involved frequent out-of-state travel with members of the opposite sex?
☐ Yes ☐ Not sure ☐ No

Would you allow your partner to take a relatively dangerous job like a police officer or roofer?
☐ Yes ☐ Not sure ☐ No

Would you delay looking for a job so that you could collect unemployment?
☐ Yes ☐ Not sure ☐ No

✫ ✫ ✫

Relatives

If you lived within an hour of your parents' residence, how many times each month would you want to see them?
    ☐ Less than 1   ☐ 1   ☐ 2–4   ☐ More than 4

How many times each month do you expect your partner to visit your family with you?
    ☐ Less than 1   ☐ 1   ☐ 2-4   ☐ More than 4

If your partner saw their parents/family much more than you saw your parents/family, would it bother you?
    ☐ Yes   ☐ Not sure   ☐ No

If one or both of your parents (or your partner's parents) became ill to the point where they could no longer take care of themselves, how would you respond?
- ☐ Let them live with us.
- ☐ Spend as much time as necessary at their house to care for them.
- ☐ Pay for home care.
- ☐ Sell their house and pay for nursing home.
- ☐ Expect other siblings/relatives to provide most of the care as I am too busy.

If one of your or your partner's family members lost their place to live, how would you respond?
- ☐ Allow them to stay with us until they get back on their feet.

- ☐ Allow them to stay with us for a limited period of time.
- ☐ Give them some money but would not provide a place to live.
- ☐ Do nothing.

How would you feel about your in-laws staying at your house for an extended visit?

- ☐ It is OK.
- ☐ I don't really welcome it, but I understand it is a part of being married.
- ☐ I can only tolerate a few days.
- ☐ Absolutely not.

How would you feel if your partner asked you to move to be closer to his or her aging parents?

- ☐ It is OK.
- ☐ I do not want to, but I will do it if there are no other options.
- ☐ I can't do it.

If a family member asked you to give them money, how would you react?

- ☐ I will give them money and maybe tell my partner later.
- ☐ I will give them money only after getting the OK from my partner.
- ☐ I will not give them any money.

✲ ✲ ✲

Food/Cooking

Whom do you expect to do most of the cooking?
  ☐ Myself   ☐ Equal share   ☐ My partner

How many nights do you expect to eat at restaurants or buy cooked food a week?
  ☐ 0–2   ☐ 3–5   ☐ 5–7

Would you rather eat out or spend money on another form of entertainment?
  ☐ Eat out   ☐ Not sure   ☐ Other form of entertainment

How many times a month do you expect to spend $100 or more for a dinner for two?
  ☐ 0–1   ☐ 2–3   ☐ More than 3

If you were cooking, would you prepare a separate meal for your spouse if he or she didn't like what you were making?
  ☐ Yes   ☐ Sometimes   ☐ No

What type of food do you like to eat at home for dinner?

☐ Chicken	☐ Salads	☐ Pork	☐ Italian
☐ Beef	☐ Casseroles	☐ Vegetarian	☐ Greek
☐ Fish	☐ Sandwiches	☐ Pizza	☐ Chinese
☐ Shellfish	☐ Hotdogs/ hamburgers	☐ Veal	☐ Other _____

FOOD/COOKING

☐ Pasta   ☐ Soup   ☐ Mexican

What type of food from the above list do you dislike?

_____   _____   _____

Would you eat something that you really didn't like for dinner if your spouse really wanted it?
☐ Yes   ☐ Sometimes   ☐ Never

Do you expect your partner to prepare your breakfast?
☐ Yes   ☐ Sometimes   ☐ No

Do you eat breakfast?
☐ Yes   ☐ Sometimes   ☐ No

Do you eat a cooked breakfast?
☐ Yes   ☐ Sometimes   ☐ No

When you have children, who will prepare breakfast?
☐ Myself   ☐ We will share   ☐ My partner

If your partner, who normally prepares breakfast or dinner, had a change in their work hours that made it inconvenient for them to do so, would you be willing to step in?
☐ Yes   ☐ Sometimes   ☐ No

How do you feel about watching television during dinner?
☐ It should never happen; dinnertime is family time.
☐ It is OK occasionally.
☐ It is fine; that is how I grew up.

✫ ✫ ✫

Sleep

What type of mattress do you prefer?
- ☐ Spring coil (☐ very firm ☐ firm ☐ plush) ☐ Pillow top
- ☐ Memory foam ☐ Sleep number/adjustable

Would you be bothered if your partner insisted on a mattress type that wasn't your first choice?
- ☐ Yes ☐ Not sure ☐ No

Which of the following describes your preferred sleep pattern?
- ☐ Go to bed early, get up early
- ☐ Go to bed late, get up late
- ☐ Go to bed anytime, get up anytime

Would you be bothered if your partner had an opposite sleep pattern from you?
- ☐ Yes ☐ Not sure ☐ No

Which of the following sleep issues apply to you?
- ☐ Snoring
- ☐ Sleep apnea
- ☐ Sleep talking
- ☐ Insomnia
- ☐ Sleep paralysis
- ☐ Need for earplugs or blindfolds

SLEEP

☐ Frequent
movements
☐ Need for
sleeping pills
☐ Frequent
nightmares

Would you be bothered if your partner had any of the sleep issues mentioned above?
☐ Yes ☐ Not sure ☐ No

If so, which ones?

_____   _____   _____

What would you do if your partner was significantly affected by one or more of the sleep issues mentioned above?
☐ Insist that my partner sleep in another room
☐ Move to another room to sleep
☐ Insist that my partner receive professional therapy
☐ Put up with it/them so we can sleep together

What size mattress do you prefer?
☐ Full ☐ Queen ☐ King

With respect to light, what type of sleep environment do you prefer?
☐ As dark as possible at night and in the morning
☐ Slight light at night, but no sunlight in morning
☐ Slight light at night, with sunlight in morning
☐ Other
☐ No preference

Would you be bothered if your partner required an opposite sleep environment from you?
☐ Yes ☐ Not sure ☐ No

With respect to temperature, what type of sleep environment do you prefer?
- ☐ Room cool, sleep under covers
- ☐ Room comfortable, sleep with little or no covers
- ☐ No preference

How long do you usually sleep on a work or school night?
- ☐ Greater than 8 hours
- ☐ 6.5 to 8 hours
- ☐ Less than 6.5 hours

How long do you usually sleep on the weekends?
- ☐ Greater than 8 hours
- ☐ 6.5 to 8 hours
- ☐ Less than 6.5 hours

If you wanted to sleep late into the morning, would it bother you if your partner was involved in an activity that was producing noise like playing loud music or running the vacuum cleaner?
- ☐ Yes   ☐ Not sure   ☐ No

✫ ✫ ✫

Past Relationships

How would you react if your partner told you he or she wanted to have lunch with an ex-relationship?
- ☐ I trust you, go right ahead.
- ☐ I don't know why you would want to do that, but I won't stop you.
- ☐ I really would rather you not do that.
- ☐ If you do that, our relationship is over.

Do you want to keep in contact with any ex-relationships?
- ☐ Yes   ☐ Not sure   ☐ No

If a person from an old relationship contacted you just to talk, how would you react?
- ☐ Stay in contact and not tell your partner, since you are not doing anything wrong
- ☐ Talk to your partner about it
- ☐ Tell your ex that you are currently in a relationship, and it would not be right to be in contact

Would you want to keep cards, letters, and photos from past relationships?
- ☐ Yes, everything
- ☐ I would like to keep some things like prom photos.
- ☐ If they bothered my partner, I would destroy everything.
- ☐ I don't have anything.

If your partner told you they wanted to keep all the cards, letters, and photos from past relationships, how would you react?
- ☐ No problem; it is the past.
- ☐ It bothers me a little, but I won't make an issue of it.
- ☐ I would want them to keep some pictures and throw away all cards and letters.
- ☐ They must throw everything away, and that is non-negotiable.

How would you react if your partner compared you to an ex-relationship?
- ☐ No big deal; it is only natural to do this.
- ☐ I'm a little upset, but I won't make an issue of it.
- ☐ I'll compare them to one of my ex-relationships.
- ☐ I'll get upset and request that it never happen again.

How would you react if your partner told you that they still "loved" a former partner but were not "in love" with them?
- ☐ I understand how they feel, and I may even feel the same way myself.
- ☐ I don't really understand it, but I know you are really in love with me now, so it is not a major issue.
- ☐ I am very bothered, and we need to have a serious talk about this.
- ☐ This will end or come close to ending our relationship.

How would you react if your partner's family compared you to a past relationship of your partner?
- ☐ I obviously don't like it, but I consider it part of the territory of being in a relationship.
- ☐ I will confront them for being rude.
- ☐ I will insist that my partner speak to their family and assure me that it won't happen again.

PAST RELATIONSHIPS

Do you believe that you can really be "just friends" with a past relationship?
    ☐ Yes   ☐ Not sure   ☐ No

How would you feel if your partner told you that he or she was thinking about hiring someone from a past relationship?
- ☐ I would be OK with it, as long as it was a good business decision.
- ☐ It would bother me, but I wouldn't stop it.
- ☐ I would not allow it.

✧ ✧ ✧

Pets

What type of pet/pets would you like to have?
- ☐ Dog
- ☐ Cat
- ☐ Bird
- ☐ Pond fish
- ☐ Horse
- ☐ Freshwater aquarium fish
- ☐ Saltwater aquarium fish
- ☐ Other_____

Would you ever have a pet that you would keep outside all the time?
- ☐ Yes
- ☐ Not sure
- ☐ No

Is there a type of pet that you are absolutely opposed to?
_____

Is there a particular type of animal you would want?
_____

If you wanted a particular pet and your partner didn't, would you be willing to take care of that pet 100% of the time?
- ☐ Yes
- ☐ Not sure
- ☐ No

Would you choose the type of house that you buy based on pet needs?
- ☐ Yes
- ☐ Not sure
- ☐ No

If you do not want a pet, what is the primary reason?
- ☐ They are too expensive to keep
- ☐ They limit your ability to travel
- ☐ They mess up the house
- ☐ I am allergic
- ☐ I just don't like animals
- ☐ We do not have time to care for them

If your partner absolutely wanted a certain pet and you didn't, how would you react?
- ☐ I allow the pet because I want to make my partner happy.
- ☐ I allow the pet, and I also expect to get or do something that my partner doesn't approve of.
- ☐ I allow the pet, but I am not happy.
- ☐ It is either me or the pet.

Would you ever allow a pet to sleep in your bed?
- ☐ Yes   ☐ Not sure   ☐ No

If you wanted a dog or a cat, would you pay extra money for a pure breed?
- ☐ Yes   ☐ Not sure   ☐ No

If circumstances rendered you unable to adequately care for your pet, what would you do?
- ☐ That would never happen.
- ☐ Find a friend or relative to care for it.
- ☐ Place it for adoption at a rescue.
- ☐ Euthanize it if there were no other options.

If you were not fond of a pet that your partner owned prior to your relationship, would you allow the pet to live with you?
    ☐ Yes   ☐ Not sure   ☐ No

If your pet became ill and required a $2,000 operation to become well, what would you do?
    ☐ Find the money and have the operation performed.
    ☐ Talk to my partner before deciding what to do.
    ☐ Strongly consider putting the animal to sleep.

Would you be interested in entering your pet in a pet show?
    ☐ Yes   ☐ Not sure   ☐ No

Would you tolerate some mess in your house to allow your pet unlimited access to the outside through a pet door?
    ☐ Yes   ☐ Not sure   ☐ No

Would you adopt a pet with a prior behavior issue?
    ☐ Yes   ☐ Not sure   ☐ No

✯ ✯ ✯

Vacations

Would you ever consider a separate vacation from your partner?
    ☐ Yes   ☐ Not sure   ☐ No

What type of vacation do you prefer?
- ☐ Relax at a beach or resort
- ☐ Cruise
- ☐ Escorted bus tour of cities/countries
- ☐ Active: hiking, biking, etc.
- ☐ Casino, shows
- ☐ Disney/theme park
- ☐ Explore other cities/countries
- ☐ Exotic, once in a lifetime
- ☐ A different type every time
- ☐ No preference
- ☐ Other_____

Are you interested in visiting the following countries, continents, and regions?

Europe	☐ Definitely	☐ Maybe	☐ Never
Asia	☐ Definitely	☐ Maybe	☐ Never
Africa/Safari	☐ Definitely	☐ Maybe	☐ Never
Australia	☐ Definitely	☐ Maybe	☐ Never

North Africa/ Middle East	☐ Definitely	☐ Maybe	☐ Never
Alaska/Canada	☐ Definitely	☐ Maybe	☐ Never
Mexico/ Caribbean	☐ Definitely	☐ Maybe	☐ Never
Pacific Islands	☐ Definitely	☐ Maybe	☐ Never
South America	☐ Definitely	☐ Maybe	☐ Never

Do you need to go on vacation every year?
    ☐ Yes   ☐ Not sure   ☐ No

How do you feel about vacations and children?
- ☐ We should enjoy some major vacations now before we have children.
- ☐ We should try to take some major vacations with the children.
- ☐ We should postpone major vacations until the children are grown and we are financially stable.

How do you feel about taking vacations with your in-laws?
- ☐ In-laws would be welcome most of the time—they make good babysitters.
- ☐ I would tolerate a few vacations with my in-laws.
- ☐ I will never go on vacation with my in-laws.

If your partner wanted to go on a type of vacation that you did not like, how would you react?
- ☐ Let's go and have a good time. After all, we will be on vacation.
- ☐ I'll go, but I expect my partner to compromise on something that he or she doesn't want to do.

VACATIONS

- ☐ I'll try to talk my partner out of going; if I don't think I'll have a good time, he or she probably won't either.
- ☐ I refuse to go.

How do you feel about going on vacation with friends?
- ☐ It is fun most of the time.
- ☐ It would be fun to do occasionally
- ☐ Those situations always lead to stress and loss of friendships.

Would you consider placing the cost of a major vacation solely on a credit card and pay for it over time?
- ☐ Yes; most people do.
- ☐ Maybe once or twice if we didn't have all the money at the time.
- ☐ Never; that practice can only get us into trouble later.

How much money should we spend on vacations every year?
- ☐ Less than $1,000
- ☐ $1,000 to $5,000
- ☐ $5,000 to $10,000
- ☐ Greater than $10,000

What is your attitude toward flying on large airplanes?
- ☐ I am fine with flying on them.
- ☐ I will travel on them, but I try to avoid them.
- ☐ I will not fly on one.

What is your attitude toward flying on small commuter airplanes?
- ☐ I am fine with flying on them.
- ☐ I will travel on them, but I try to avoid them.
- ☐ I will not go on one.

What is your attitude toward traveling on large cruise ships?
- ☐ I am fine with traveling on them.
- ☐ I am somewhat uncomfortable on them, but I will go on one if my partner really wants to.
- ☐ I will not go on one.

Would you ever consider buying a boat?
☐ Yes   ☐ Not sure   ☐ No

Would you purchase a vacation home for your major vacations?
☐ Yes   ☐ Not sure   ☐ No

Would you invest in a 'time share" for your major vacations?
☐ Yes   ☐ Not sure   ☐ No

☆ ☆ ☆

Holidays

What do you like to do on New Year's Eve?
   ☐ Go to a party   ☐ It doesn't matter   ☐ Stay at home

How would you like to spend the Thanksgiving holiday as a couple?
   ☐ I want to always have dinner at my home.
   ☐ I want to always have dinner at my parents' home.
   ☐ I want to alternate having dinner at my parents' home, my partner's parents' home, and maybe sometimes at my home.
   ☐ It is all too much trouble; I would like to go to a restaurant most of the time.

How do you feel about decorating your home for holidays?
   ☐ I enjoy it very much, and it is very important to me for all holidays.
   ☐ I like to do it for major holidays only.
   ☐ It doesn't matter to me—my partner can do it as long as it doesn't cost too much.
   ☐ It is a waste of time and money.

How would you like to spend the major religious holidays?
- ☐ At our home with the children
- ☐ At my parent's home
- ☐ Different places, depending on the status of children
- ☐ It doesn't matter to me

How do you feel about going on vacation during the major holidays?
- ☐ I will do it anytime my partner wants to.
- ☐ I would do it occasionally.
- ☐ I am against it. Holidays are not for vacations.

How do you feel about sending out greeting cards during holidays?
- ☐ I enjoy doing it.
- ☐ I like it, as long as my partner does most of it.
- ☐ It is a waste of time and money.

✭ ✭ ✭

Hobbies

List your three favorite hobbies:
_____   _____   _____

How much money per year would you spend on hobbies?
☐ Less than $500   ☐ $500 to $2,000   ☐ Greater than $2,000

How do you feel about the equity of both partners in the relationship spending money on hobbies?
☐ My partner should spend as much as he or she requires to make him or her happy.
☐ We don't have to spend precisely the same amount, but we should set a household budget for hobbies.
☐ Both of us should establish a budget for spending the same amount of money on hobbies.
☐ At this stage in our life, there are better things to spend money on.

How do you feel about getting your partner interested in your hobbies?
☐ I welcome that.
☐ Some occasional involvement would be nice.
☐ Hobbies are meant to be enjoyed with people other than my partner.

How would you react if your partner wanted to spend a large amount of money on a hobby-related item that you are not interested in (e.g., $5,000 for a telescope) and pay for the purchase with a credit card?
- ☐ That's OK.
- ☐ Sure, and I want to charge the same amount on something for myself.
- ☐ I allow it only if they save for it, and I would not allow it to be charged.
- ☐ I do not allow it; that is too much money to charge.

How would you feel if your partner decided to participate in a dangerous hobby such as mountain climbing?
- ☐ I'm fine with whatever makes them happy.
- ☐ I will try to discourage it, but ultimately it is their decision.
- ☐ It could end our relationship.

✫ ✫ ✫

Religion

Which best describes your religious beliefs and behavior?
- ☐ I believe in God, am part of an organized religion, and attend services regularly.
- ☐ I believe in God, am part of an organized religion, and attend services occasionally.
- ☐ I believe in God, am supposed to be part of an organized religion, but rarely attend services.
- ☐ I am agnostic.
- ☐ I am spiritual but do not believe in organized religion.
- ☐ I am an atheist.

How important is it that your partner have the same attitude toward religion as you do?
- ☐ Very important ☐ Somewhat important ☐ Not important

How important is it that your partner belong to the same organized religion as you do?
- ☐ Very important ☐ Somewhat important ☐ Not important

How important is it that your children are raised in your religion?
- ☐ Very important ☐ Somewhat important ☐ Not important

Would you ever consider converting to your partner's religion?
- ☐ Yes   ☐ Not sure   ☐ No   ☐ Not applicable

Would it bother you if you were asked to raise your children in your partner's religion?
☐ Yes ☐ Not sure ☐ No ☐ Not applicable

How much money do you expect to contribute to your organized religion each year?
☐ None ☐ Less than $500
☐ $500–1,500 ☐ Greater than $1,500

Is it important to you to live in a neighborhood with other families of the same religion as you?
☐ Yes ☐ Not sure ☐ No

Do you believe in trying to convert others to the same religion as you?
☐ Yes ☐ Not sure ☐ No

Would you ever want to hold religious meetings in your home?
☐ Yes ☐ Not sure ☐ No

Would you ever want to go on a religious vacation?
☐ Yes ☐ Not sure ☐ No

How do you feel about having religious pictures, statues, or artifacts in your home?
☐ They are important to me; I want some in my home.
☐ I would consider having a few if my partner wanted them.
☐ I do not want any.

Do you believe in the power of prayer?
☐ Yes ☐ Not sure ☐ No

Do you believe in miracles?

☐ Yes ☐ Not sure ☐ No

Which of the following theories regarding the origin of life do you believe?

☐ Creationism
☐ Intelligent design
☐ Evolution

How do you feel about religious greeting cards?

☐ They are important to me.
☐ It doesn't matter to me.
☐ I don't like them.

✡ ✡ ✡

School/Education

Do you plan on furthering your education at some time in the future?
 ☐ Yes   ☐ Not sure   ☐ No

Do you expect your partner to further his or her education so that he or she can get a better job?
 ☐ Yes   ☐ Not sure   ☐ No

Are you willing to make short-term sacrifices like working two jobs or living with parents so that your partner can go to school to have a better job in the future?
 ☐ Yes   ☐ Not sure   ☐ No

Are you willing to live in a smaller house so your children could be in a better school system?
 ☐ Yes   ☐ Not sure   ☐ No

Are you be willing to make severe financial and lifestyle sacrifices so that your children can go to private schools?
 ☐ Yes   ☐ Not sure   ☐ No

Do you expect your parents (or your partner's parents) to help with your children's college education?
 ☐ Yes ☐ Not sure ☐ No ☐ Not applicable

Which of the following best describes your attitude toward establishing a college fund for your children?
 ☐ It is a major priority.

SCHOOL/EDUCATION

☐ I expect to have some money set aside to pay for part of their education.
☐ I had to pay for my own education, and I expect my children to do the same.

Which of the following best describes your attitude toward influencing your child toward a particular career?
☐ I expect them to take over the family business.
☐ I would like them to pursue the same career path that I did.
☐ Whatever they do is fine, as long as they choose a career that allows them to make an adequate salary.
☐ Their career choice is entirely up to them.

Would you ever consider withholding college fund money if your child wanted to pursue an area of study that you did not agree with?
☐ Yes ☐ Not sure ☐ No

Will you encourage your child to go out of state to college for more life experience?
☐ Yes ☐ Not sure ☐ No

Will you encourage your child to attend a local college to remain close to you or to save on living expenses?
☐ Yes ☐ Not sure ☐ No

Do you think the theory of evolution should be taught to your children?
☐ Yes ☐ Not sure ☐ No

✯ ✯ ✯

Health

What is your general attitude toward health?
- ☐ It is the most important thing in life, and I will always try to exercise, eat right, sleep right, and make medical appointments for preventive health.
- ☐ It is important, and I try to incorporate proper diet, exercise, and prevention into my busy routine.
- ☐ There needs to be a balance between living healthy and enjoying life.
- ☐ You only live once, so enjoy your time to the fullest.

If your partner's attitude toward health is very different than yours, what will you do?
- ☐ There is not much you can do—it is their life.
- ☐ I'll try to persuade them to change by setting an example.
- ☐ I'll insist on certain changes.

Do you believe in the medical benefit of vaccination?
- ☐ Yes   ☐ Not sure   ☐ No

Do you believe in living wills, "do not resuscitate" orders, and hospice care?
- ☐ Yes, there is no need for unnecessary suffering at the end of life.
- ☐ Only in extreme circumstances.
- ☐ No, God should decide when the end of life comes.

HEALTH

Will you make it a point to encourage your children to live a healthier lifestyle than you do?
    ☐ Yes   ☐ Not sure   ☐ No   ☐ Not applicable

Do you believe in the health benefits of high doses of vitamins?
    ☐ Yes   ☐ Not sure   ☐ No

Do you believe in alternative medicine approaches to serious diseases like cancer?
    ☐ Yes   ☐ Not sure   ☐ No

Do you believe in preventive medicine?
    ☐ Yes   ☐ Not sure   ☐ No

Would you ever not take medicine prescribed to you by a medical doctor because it was too expensive?
    ☐ Yes   ☐ Not sure   ☐ No

Would you ever not have health insurance because it is too expensive?
    ☐ Yes   ☐ Not sure   ☐ No

✯ ✯ ✯

Sports

What sports do you like to play?
_____   _____   _____

What sports do you like to watch?
_____   _____   _____

Is it important that your partner is interested in the same sports as you?
    ☐ Yes   ☐ Not sure   ☐ No

How much money do you spend a year on expenses related to sports participation?
    ☐ Less than $500   ☐ $500–1,500   ☐ Greater than $1,500

How much money do you spend a year on expenses related to spectator sports (not counting those related to your children)?
    ☐ Less than $500   ☐ $500–1,500   ☐ Greater than $1,500

Would you ever place your desire to participate in or to watch certain sports ahead of family matters/events?
    ☐ Yes   ☐ Not sure   ☐ No

Would you ever insist that your children play a certain sport if they were not interested in playing?
    ☐ Yes   ☐ Not sure   ☐ No

SPORTS

Would you spend $500 or more for sports memorabilia?
☐ Yes ☐ Not sure ☐ No

✭ ✭ ✭

House/Home Life

Where do you prefer to live?
    ☐ City   ☐ Suburb   ☐ Rural   ☐ Doesn't matter

Which would you prefer?
    ☐ Larger house, less spending money
    ☐ Smaller house, more spending money
    ☐ Not sure

Do you prefer?
    ☐ Ranch home   ☐ Two-story home
    ☐ Condominium   ☐ Not sure

Which of the following must you have in your house?
- ☐ Open floor plan
- ☐ Nice views
- ☐ Large kitchen
- ☐ Large yard
- ☐ Pool
- ☐ Ranch style
- ☐ More than two bathrooms
- ☐ Four bedrooms
- ☐ Large walk-in closet
- ☐ Two stories
- ☐ Associated with good school system
- ☐ Close to public transportation
- ☐ Close to place of employment
- ☐ Close to family
- ☐ Finished basement
- ☐ In-law suite
- ☐ Secluded location
- ☐ Whirlpool tub in bathroom

What is your attitude toward a home mortgage?
    ☐ Large down payment, pay off as fast as possible
    ☐ Normal down payment, pay off in thirty years

HOUSE/HOME LIFE

- ☐ Normal down payment, pay off in fifteen years
- ☐ Smallest down payment, refinance to extend payoff as long as possible

Which of the following best describes your attitude toward your first home?
- ☐ Rent until we can afford our dream home
- ☐ Buy a small starter home or condominium first, then buy a better home in the future
- ☐ Rent, buy a starter home, and then buy better homes if able
- ☐ Always live in a condominium

Who will make the majority of the decisions regarding the interior decorating?
- ☐ I will
- ☐ Both of us will discuss and compromise
- ☐ My partner will
- ☐ I would like to hire a decorator

Whom do you envision cleaning the inside of the home?
- ☐ Me
- ☐ Both of us
- ☐ My partner
- ☐ Neither of us: I want to hire a cleaning service or maid

Whom do you envision taking care of the landscaping/cutting the grass?
- ☐ Me
- ☐ Both of us
- ☐ My partner
- ☐ Neither of us: I want to hire a contractor

Whom do you envision doing snow removal at your home?
- ☐ Me
- ☐ Both of us
- ☐ My partner
- ☐ Neither of us: I want to hire a contractor

Which of the following best describes your attitude toward the ideal organization of the inside of the home?
- ☐ Everything should have its place; it should look like a museum.
- ☐ It should be neat and organized most of the time.
- ☐ It is impossible to keep it neat, so why bother?

Who will do your laundry?
- ☐ I will
- ☐ Sometimes me, sometimes my partner
- ☐ My partner

Would you consider having a gun in your home for security?
- ☐ Yes ☐ Not sure ☐ No

Which of the following must you have at your home?
- ☐ Exercise equipment
- ☐ Sit-down bar
- ☐ Kids' play room
- ☐ Vegetable garden
- ☐ Pool table
- ☐ Home theater
- ☐ Hot tub
- ☐ Home office
- ☐ Pond
- ☐ Wine cellar

What color kitchen cabinets do you prefer?
- ☐ Light wood
- ☐ Other
- ☐ Dark wood
- ☐ No preference

HOUSE/HOME LIFE

What type of home decorating do you prefer?
 □ Traditional □ Eclectic □ Contemporary □ other

Do you like to play loud music at home?
 □ Yes   □ Sometimes   □ No

Do you have trouble throwing things away?
 □ Yes   □ Sometimes   □ No

✫ ✫ ✫

Marriage Ceremony

Do you want a formal marriage ceremony?
    ☐ Yes   ☐ Not sure   ☐ No   ☐ Not applicable

How much do you want to spend on a marriage ceremony/reception?
    ☐ Less than $10,00   ☐ $10,000–30,000   ☐ Greater than $30,000

How do you expect to pay for a marriage ceremony/reception?
- ☐ The bride's parents will pay.
- ☐ The parents of both partners will pay.
- ☐ Our parents will pay and we will also contribute.
- ☐ We will pay.

Which is the most important with regards to money at the beginning of a marriage?
- ☐ Spend money on the ceremony/reception
- ☐ Spend money on the rings
- ☐ Spend money on the honeymoon
- ☐ Save money for the future

Do you want a traditional wedding reception with the usual expenses of photographer, cake, wedding dress, food/drink, reception hall, and band?
    ☐ Yes   ☐ Not sure   ☐ No

MARRIAGE CEREMONY

Would you ever consider eloping?
 ☐ Yes   ☐ Not sure   ☐ No

What are the elements of your ideal wedding reception?

Location _____

Number of guests _____

Food	☐ Sit-down dinner	☐ Buffet	☐ Light hors d'oeuvres only
Drink	☐ Open bar	☐ Cash bar	☐ No alcoholic beverages
Dress	☐ Budget	☐ Up to $1,500	☐ Greater than $1,500
Music	☐ Disc jockey	☐ Live band	☐ Other
Images	☐ Professional photographer and videographer	☐ Photographer only	☐ Other

✫ ✫ ✫

Appearance

Would you ever ask your partner to do any of the following?
- ☐ Dye their hair
- ☐ Lose weight
- ☐ Wear a hairpiece
- ☐ Get cosmetic surgery or use Botox.
- ☐ Get dental work
- ☐ Wear more conservative clothes
- ☐ Wear more provocative clothes
- ☐ Wear a different cologne or perfume

How would you react if your partner asked you to do one or more of the above to improve your appearance?
- ☐ I'll do it.
- ☐ I'll consider some things, but I'm a little bothered.
- ☐ You should be happy with me the way that I am.

How would you react if your partner's appearance dramatically changed in a year or two due to overeating and lack of exercise?
- ☐ I love you the way you are.
- ☐ I'll try to get you to change your habits.
- ☐ It could end the relationship.

✯ ✯ ✯

Shopping

Do you enjoy shopping?
    ☐ Yes   ☐ Sometimes   ☐ No

Is it important that your partner go shopping with you?
    ☐ Yes   ☐ Sometimes   ☐ No

Whom do you envision doing the grocery shopping?
    ☐ I will   ☐ Both of us   ☐ My partner

Is there any shopping that you absolutely must be a part of?
    ☐ Yes   ☐ Not sure   ☐ No

If so, what?_____

Would it bother you if your partner excessively used coupons?
    ☐ Yes   ☐ Not sure   ☐ No

Would it bother if your partner always wanted to find the cheapest price?
    ☐ Yes   ☐ Not sure   ☐ No

✭ ✭ ✭

Addictions

Which of the following do you enjoy?
- ☐ Drinking alcohol
- ☐ Gambling
- ☐ Taking recreational drugs
- ☐ Smoking cigarettes
- ☐ Surfing the Internet
- ☐ Watching television
- ☐ Playing video games

How many alcohol drinks a week (one drink is considered a 12 oz. beer, a shot, or a glass of wine) would you tolerate your partner consuming before it would bother you?
- ☐ Any amount would bother me
- ☐ Seven
- ☐ Fourteen
- ☐ Twenty-one
- ☐ He or she can drink any amount as long as they can function at home and at work.

How much time would you tolerate your partner spending on the Internet each day for non-business-related activities before it would bother you? _____ .

How much time would you tolerate your partner spending each day playing video games without you before it would bother you? _____ .

How much money would you allow your partner to lose per year on gambling before it would bother you? _____ .

ADDICTIONS

How much time per week would you tolerate your partner watching television you didn't want to watch before it would bother you? _____ .

If you are a smoker, when do you intend to quit?
- ☐ In the immediate future
- ☐ I tried in the past, and I will try again soon
- ☐ I don't want to quit now

If you are a smoker, do you smoke in the house?
☐ Yes ☐ Sometimes ☐ No

If you enjoy alcohol, is it important that your partner enjoys it with you?
☐ Yes ☐ Sometimes ☐ No

If you found out that your partner had a past problem with addictions but is fine now, would it bother you?
☐ Yes ☐ Not sure ☐ No

✭ ✭ ✭

Intimacy

Do you like to hold hands in public?
  ☐ Yes   ☐ Sometimes   ☐ No

Do you like to cuddle while sleeping?
  ☐ Yes   ☐ Sometimes   ☐ No

How would you react if you found out your partner went to a gentlemen's club or male stripper club?
  ☐ It's not a big deal; I know he or she loves me.
  ☐ I am OK with it as long as it is not on a regular basis.
  ☐ It bothers me, and I need to talk with my partner about why they do it.
  ☐ It could end the relationship if it happens again.

How would you react if you found out that your partner was talking to "singles looking to meet other singles" in an Internet chat room?
  ☐ It's not a big deal—those places are just a joke, and I know he or she loves me.
  ☐ It bothers me, and I need to know that it won't happen again.
  ☐ I consider it cheating, and it could end the relationship.

During intimate moments, would you like to see your partner be more expressive of his or her feelings?
  ☐ Yes   ☐ Sometimes   ☐ No

INTIMACY

Is there something your partner can do to improve the intimacy between you?
    ☐ Yes   ☐ Not sure   ☐ No

If you answered *Yes* above, explain here. _____
_____

Do you feel that "absence makes the heart grow fonder"?
    ☐ Yes   ☐ Sometimes   ☐ No

How important is "complete truthfulness" to a relationship?
- ☐ Nothing is more important.
- ☐ No one can tell the truth all the time; the occasional white lie is OK.
- ☐ How I treat someone is more important than what I say to them.

How would you react if your partner wanted you both to seek professional help for intimacy issues in the relationship?
- ☐ I would go. It could help our relationship.
- ☐ I would feel awkward, but I would go.
- ☐ I would refuse to go.

✯ ✯ ✯

Politics

How would you describe your political views?
- ☐ Very conservative ☐ Conservative ☐ Middle
- ☐ Liberal ☐ Very liberal ☐ Mixed

Is it important that your partner share the same political views as you?
- ☐ Yes ☐ Not sure ☐ No

Would you ever volunteer to campaign for a political candidate?
- ☐ Yes ☐ Not sure ☐ No

Would you ever join a peaceful protest?
- ☐ Yes ☐ Not sure ☐ No

Would you try to influence your children to have your political views?
- ☐ Yes ☐ Not sure ☐ No

Would you try to influence your partner's voting?
- ☐ Yes ☐ Not sure ☐ No

✯ ✯ ✯

Time

How much time would your partner have to spend in the bathroom in the morning for it to bother you? _____.

How would you react if your partner was frequently five to fifteen minutes late for events?
- ☐ It's not a big deal.
- ☐ It bothers me, but there is nothing I can do to change them.
- ☐ It could end the relationship.

What is your philosophy toward time management?
- ☐ I always try to be early.
- ☐ I always try to arrive on time.
- ☐ I am always on "island time." Life is too short to stress out over time.

✭ ✭ ✭

Friends

Do you expect your partner to like most of your friends?
    ☐ Yes   ☐ Not sure   ☐ No

Would it bother you if your partner had a good friend who had a criminal past?
    ☐ Yes   ☐ Not sure   ☐ No

Would it bother you if your partner had a good friend who had an ongoing addiction?
    ☐ Yes   ☐ Not sure   ☐ No

Would it bother you if your partner had a good friend who was an atheist?
    ☐ Yes   ☐ Not sure   ☐ No

Would it bother you if your partner had a good friend who was a persistent cheater in relationships?
    ☐ Yes   ☐ Not sure   ☐ No

How many times a month would you allow your partner to go out with his or her friends without you before it would bother you?
    ☐ 0   ☐ 1   ☐ 2-4   ☐ 5 or greater

FRIENDS

Would you allow your partner to go without you to a single's bar or club with single friends?
    ☐ Yes   ☐ Not sure   ☐ No

Would you travel a long distance without your partner to visit friends?
    ☐ Yes   ☐ Not sure   ☐ No

If you noticed your partner staring at an attractive friend of yours, how would you react?
- ☐ It's not a big deal.
- ☐ It would bother me a little, but it is not worth arguing about.
- ☐ It is disrespectful, and must stop.

✫ ✫ ✫

Miscellaneous

Do you believe in ghosts?
    ☐ Yes   ☐ Not sure   ☐ No

Do you believe in energy sources that modern science can't explain?
    ☐ Yes   ☐ Not sure   ☐ No

Do you believe that certain groups of humans are superior to others?
    ☐ Yes   ☐ Not sure   ☐ No

Do you believe what you are told in infomercials?
    ☐ Yes   ☐ Sometimes   ☐ No

Do you believe in luck?
    ☐ Yes   ☐ Not sure   ☐ No

Do you believe that everything happens for a reason?
    ☐ Yes   ☐ Not sure   ☐ No

Do you believe that all occurrences are random events?
    ☐ Yes   ☐ Not sure   ☐ No

D you believe in UFOs?
    ☐ Yes   ☐ Not sure   ☐ No

MISCELLANEOUS

Do you believe in hypnosis as a means of therapy?
☐ Yes   ☐ Not sure   ☐ No

Do you believe in astrology and psychics?
☐ Yes   ☐ Not sure   ☐ No

Do you believe in reincarnation?
☐ Yes   ☐ Not sure   ☐ No

If applicable, will you take the last name of your partner?
☐ Yes
☐ No, I want to keep my name.
☐ I want to hyphenate both names.
☐ Not applicable

Will you ask your partner to take dance lessons?
☐ Yes   ☐ Not sure   ☐ No

✯ ✯ ✯

Part B

Directions

This book consists of two identical parts labeled Part A and Part B.

Ideally, both partners should complete this exercise at the same time. It should take about an hour or so to answer the questions, and then both partners should review their answers with each other and have a discussion.

To begin, you must rip the book in half. Find the middle of the book where Part B begins, fold the book back and forth several times vertically so that there is a significant crease in the side binding of the book, and then gently rip the book into two parts. You will not need to use anything but your fingers. Each partner then takes a book part and begins the exercise, and hopefully, you will be on your way to a **win-win** relationship.

Introduction

I am not a psychologist, psychiatrist or relationship expert. I am a physician and a scientist who has spent almost forty years as an adult watching the same roller-coaster pattern of relationship deterioration over and over again. It goes something like this:

1. You see someone that you are attracted to.
2. You meet them.
3. You date.
4. The neurotransmitters in your brain trigger so much pleasure that attention and critical thinking are impaired.
5. You can't get enough of the other person.
6. You decide to get married or live together, thinking that the "happy" neurotransmitters will stimulate your brain for the rest of your life.
7. Everyday issues lead to minor conflicts.
8. Your partner reacts to these conflicts in an unanticipated and sometimes confrontational way.
9. You become confused and don't understand this behavior.
10. Time goes by and these negative encounters become more frequent.
11. You convince yourself that your partner has changed.
12. As more time passes, you lose all sense of happiness with the relationship.
13. You avoid communication as a defense measure.
14. The relationship remains at this low level or ends.

INTRODUCTION

Sound familiar? What happened? I believe a major part of the answer lies with **expectations**. When a relationship is flying high, we engage in subconscious (and sometimes conscious) assumptions about our partner to avoid the interruption of the "feel good" neurotransmitters. We conclude, "If my partner loves me, he or she must agree with everything about me, including my quirky habits, beliefs, ethics, and everyday behaviors." So when we are finally confronted with the reality that we differ from our partner over an issue, we become disappointed because our **expectations** have been shattered. Thus begins the negative tailspin.

What can you do? You could see a relationship counselor, but I believe a more logical approach, consistent with modern trends in twenty-first century medicine, is one of prevention. If couples understand early in the relationship how their partners think about numerous everyday issues that could arise in the future, then the negative energy and feelings from broken **expectations** could be minimized, and replaced with the positive energy of **compromise**. When a conflicting issue surfaces, if you already know what your partner's reaction is going to be, you can offer a **compromise** instead of an argument.

When you think about it, we spend the entire day resolving minor conflicts in our personal lives by making **compromise** decisions. *Should I buy this or save the money? Should I wear a tie or be more comfortable without?* Since we know all about us, it is easy to make a balanced **compromise** decision that maximizes the positive and minimizes the negative aspects of our choice. This is a **win-win** decision—the gold standard for conflict resolution. Your goal is to have **win-win** relationship interactions in which you and your partner feel good about the result, and the positive energy keeps flowing.

This book consists of a series of questions relating to common issues that come up in the course of two people being together in a committed relationship. They are grouped into categories in no special order. Obviously, not all questions will be relevant to any one relationship, but you should answer most. It is my hope that this book will be a significant catalyst for a "couple discovery" process. After dividing the book into its two identical parts, both partners should answer all of the questions alone.

After completion, the couple should come together and go over the questions one by one. Hopefully this will lead to some meaningful relationship insight, some resolution of controversial issues, and some good, old-fashioned fun.

I must caution you that this question book has never been formally tested, and there is the possibility of a negative outcome for some couples, so proceed at your own risk. If you have significant problems compromising, you should consider: 1) Bringing the results of this exercise to a couples' counselor, or 2) Reading other books on compromising skills. I think that the majority of couples will have more positive than negative results from the exercise as long as you set aside your **expectations**, think **compromise**, and aim for **win-win** outcomes.

Topics

Children	67
Money	70
Employment	73
Relatives	76
Food/Cooking	78
Sleep	80
Past Relationships	83
Pets	86
Vacations	89
Holidays	93
Hobbies	95
Religion	97
School/Education	100
Health	102
Sports	104
House/Home Life	106
Marriage Ceremony	110
Appearance	112
Shopping	113
Addictions	114
Intimacy	116
Politics	118
Time	119
Friends	120
Miscellaneous	122

Disclaimer

This book is for entertainment purposes only. It is not meant to provide relationship counseling, and it cannot diagnose and treat any psychological condition or disease. Neither the author nor the publisher can be responsible for any damages that are perceived to result from the use of this book.

Children

How many children do you want to have? _____

If you couldn't have children, would you consider:
    Adoption? ☐ Yes ☐ Not sure ☐ No
    In-vitro fertilization? ☐ Yes ☐ Not sure ☐ No
    Surrogate mother? ☐ Yes ☐ Not sure ☐ No
    Sperm bank? ☐ Yes ☐ Not sure ☐ No

Would you keep having children to have one of the opposite sex?
    ☐ Yes ☐ Not sure ☐ No

At what age would you like to start having children? _____

At what age would you like to stop having children? _____

If you had an ectopic pregnancy, would you want to continue to have children?
    ☐ Yes ☐ Not sure ☐ No

If you were told you were going to have a child with Down Syndrome, would you keep the child?
    ☐ Yes ☐ Not sure ☐ No

If you had a seriously autistic child, would you consider placing the child in an institution?
    ☐ Yes ☐ Not sure ☐ No

What kind of school do you prefer that your children attend?
- ☐ Public school
- ☐ Private religious school
- ☐ Private school
- ☐ Home school

Do you believe in spanking children?
- ☐ Yes, that's how I was raised
- ☐ Sometimes, in extreme circumstances
- ☐ Never

How would you feel about your children trying out for contact sports?
- ☐ Whatever they would want to do is fine
- ☐ Yes, but not football or hockey
- ☐ No contact sports

At what age would you allow your child to sleep over a friend's house?
- ☐ 4–5
- ☐ 10–11
- ☐ 6–7
- ☐ 12–13
- ☐ 8–9
- ☐ Never

Whom would you allow to babysit your child?
- ☐ Close family and friends
- ☐ Only referred adults
- ☐ Referred adults and teenagers
- ☐ Nobody

Which of the following best describes your attitude toward having adult children living with you in your home?
- ☐ They can stay as long as they want.
- ☐ They can stay for a year or two, until they save enough money for a place of their own.
- ☐ They are adults, and they need to make whatever sacrifices it takes to live on their own; allowing them to live with me would do more harm than good.

CHILDREN

If you and your partner will be traveling on a plane without your children, do you believe in taking separate planes?
 ☐ Yes   ☐ Not sure   ☐ No

Would it bother you if your partner insisted on naming your child after themselves or their parents?
 ☐ Yes   ☐ Not sure   ☐ No

Would you ever want to enter your young child in a pageant or talent contest?
 ☐ Yes   ☐ Not sure   ☐ No

How would you react if your child told you that they were going to enlist in the military?
 ☐ I support it. It is a very honorable thing to do.
 ☐ I do not support it, but I will not stop it.
 ☐ I will do everything possible to discourage it.

Would you want to send your children to a camp for part of the summer?
 ☐ Yes   ☐ Not sure   ☐ No

Would you ever want to send your children to stay with relatives for part of the summer?
 ☐ Yes   ☐ Not sure   ☐ No

✫ ✫ ✫

Money

Who will manage the money in the household?
  ☐ Myself   ☐ My partner   ☐ Both of us

What type of banking arrangement do you envision?
  ☐ One account: everything comes from it
  ☐ Separate accounts: one partner pays for certain things, and the other partner pays for other things
  ☐ Three accounts: one for all household expenses, and separate personal accounts for each partner
  ☐ Other

In order of importance, rank your five top priorities for spending money:
  __Home   __Home furnishings   __Vacations
  __Personal education
  __Entertainment (movies, cable, sports, shows)
  __Children's education   __Nice cars
  __Drinking/drugs   __Gambling
  __Investments __Restaurants
  __Retirement savings   __Children's college savings
  __New clothing   __Jewelry   __Gifts to family
  __Child expenses (clothes, toys, classes, parties, etc.)
  _____Other

How much of your combined income would you like to donate to charity?
  ☐ None   ☐ About 1%   ☐ 1–3%
  ☐ 3–5%   ☐ Greater than 5%

If one of us works and the other manages the home, how will we make decisions regarding money?
- ☐ The working person will be the decision maker, and the other partner will need permission to spend money.
- ☐ The working person will pay all the bills and allow the other a monthly allowance of money for personal spending.
- ☐ Both partners will always have a say in how we spend money.
- ☐ Other

How much credit card debt is too much?
- ☐ Over $1,000 ☐ Over $5,000 ☐ Over $10,000
- ☐ Over $20,000

Would you ever consider bankruptcy?
- ☐ Yes ☐ Not sure ☐ No

If you found out that your partner took out a credit card without your knowledge and owed over $5,000 on it, how would you react?
- ☐ I expect them to pay it off as soon as possible.
- ☐ I am upset about the secrecy.
- ☐ It could end the relationship.

How do you feel about spending money on children?
- ☐ My children will have whatever they want.
- ☐ My children will get presents on birthdays/holidays, and a weekly allowance.
- ☐ My children will get presents on birthdays/holidays, and a weekly allowance in exchange for doing chores.
- ☐ My children will get some presents, but they will be expected to help around the house for no allowance.

Which of the following best describes your attitude toward spending money?
- ☐ Pay for everything in cash except your house and car, and avoid debt at all costs.
- ☐ It is normal and acceptable to have some credit card debt.
- ☐ You are only young once and could be dead tomorrow, so don't deny yourself anything that can be bought on credit.

Which of the following best describes your attitude toward investing money?
- ☐ I want my money either in low risk CDs or at home in my mattress.
- ☐ I would like the customary level of investment risk for my age.
- ☐ I believe in a high-risk, high reward strategy. You can't get rich by leaving your money in the bank.

Would you ever want to invest in real estate and become a landlord?
    ☐ Yes   ☐ Not sure   ☐ No

Do you like to invest in common stocks that you pick yourself?
    ☐ Yes   ☐ Sometimes   ☐ No

✭ ✭ ✭

Employment

Would you consider a job opportunity that involved significant (greater than 50 % of the time) long- distance travel?
    ☐ Yes   ☐ Not sure   ☐ No

If you were happy in a location and your children were in the local school system, would you consider moving to another state so that either you or your partner could have a better employment opportunity?
    ☐ Yes   ☐ Not sure   ☐ No

How would you feel if your partner was considering a promotion that involved a 40% raise but required a 50–60 hour work week with weekend work?
- ☐ I welcome it and will modify our lifestyle accordingly.
- ☐ I don't like it, but I am willing to give it a try for a year or two to see if we can adapt.
- ☐ I am against it. Family time and lack of stress are more important than the extra money.

If your partner was the primary income producer and lost his or her job, would you be willing to work extra—or even two jobs—until he or she found another job in their field?
- ☐ Yes.
- ☐ Yes, but after a while I would expect them to find some type of job to help out.

☐ No, my partner should take any job he could find while looking for a job in his area. I should not be expected to work more.

Imagine that your partner is the primary income producer and has a good job and benefits. If he or she suddenly decided to leave his or her employment and start his or her own company, knowing the risks and financial struggles, how would you react?
☐ I completely support him or her. Owning one's own business is the American dream.
☐ I will only support it if the sacrifice is not too great, and I will only give it a limited period of time to work out.
☐ I am against it, as the risk is too great. In these times, you should be happy you have a good job with good benefits.

In a family with young children, do you consider it important for one of the parents to not work and stay at home?
☐ Yes   ☐ Not sure   ☐ No

Which of the following best describes your philosophy?
☐ Work hard, invest in the future
☐ Work hard, play hard
☐ Work enough to get by; time for family and friends is most important
☐ You are only young once; do whatever you have to do to get by, and work only when you have to

Would you allow your partner to take a job that involved working predominately with members of the opposite sex?
☐ Yes   ☐ Not sure   ☐ No

EMPLOYMENT

Would you allow your partner to take a job that involved frequent out-of-state travel with members of the opposite sex?
☐ Yes ☐ Not sure ☐ No

Would you allow your partner to take a relatively dangerous job like a police officer or roofer?
☐ Yes ☐ Not sure ☐ No

Would you delay looking for a job so that you could collect unemployment?
☐ Yes ☐ Not sure ☐ No

✩ ✩ ✩

Relatives

If you lived within an hour of your parents' residence, how many times each month would you want to see them?
 ☐ Less than 1 ☐ 1 ☐ 2–4 ☐ More than 4

How many times each month do you expect your partner to visit your family with you?
 ☐ Less than 1 ☐ 1 ☐ 2-4 ☐ More than 4

If your partner saw their parents/family much more than you saw your parents/family, would it bother you?
 ☐ Yes ☐ Not sure ☐ No

If one or both of your parents (or your partner's parents) became ill to the point where they could no longer take care of themselves, how would you respond?
- ☐ Let them live with us.
- ☐ Spend as much time as necessary at their house to care for them.
- ☐ Pay for home care.
- ☐ Sell their house and pay for nursing home.
- ☐ Expect other siblings/relatives to provide most of the care as I am too busy.

If one of your or your partner's family members lost their place to live, how would you respond?
- ☐ Allow them to stay with us until they get back on their feet.

RELATIVES

- ☐ Allow them to stay with us for a limited period of time.
- ☐ Give them some money but would not provide a place to live.
- ☐ Do nothing.

How would you feel about your in-laws staying at your house for an extended visit?
- ☐ It is OK.
- ☐ I don't really welcome it, but I understand it is a part of being married.
- ☐ I can only tolerate a few days.
- ☐ Absolutely not.

How would you feel if your partner asked you to move to be closer to his or her aging parents?
- ☐ It is OK.
- ☐ I do not want to, but I will do it if there are no other options.
- ☐ I can't do it.

If a family member asked you to give them money, how would you react?
- ☐ I will give them money and maybe tell my partner later.
- ☐ I will give them money only after getting the OK from my partner.
- ☐ I will not give them any money.

✫ ✫ ✫

Food/Cooking

Whom do you expect to do most of the cooking?
☐ Myself ☐ Equal share ☐ My partner

How many nights do you expect to eat at restaurants or buy cooked food a week?
☐ 0–2 ☐ 3–5 ☐ 5–7

Would you rather eat out or spend money on another form of entertainment?
☐ Eat out ☐ Not sure ☐ Other form of entertainment

How many times a month do you expect to spend $100 or more for a dinner for two?
☐ 0–1 ☐ 2–3 ☐ More than 3

If you were cooking, would you prepare a separate meal for your spouse if he or she didn't like what you were making?
☐ Yes ☐ Sometimes ☐ No

What type of food do you like to eat at home for dinner?

☐ Chicken	☐ Salads	☐ Pork	☐ Italian
☐ Beef	☐ Casseroles	☐ Vegetarian	☐ Greek
☐ Fish	☐ Sandwiches	☐ Pizza	☐ Chinese
☐ Shellfish	☐ Hotdogs/ hamburgers	☐ Veal	☐ Other _____

FOOD/COOKING

☐ Pasta   ☐ Soup   ☐ Mexican

What type of food from the above list do you dislike?
_____ _____ _____

Would you eat something that you really didn't like for dinner if your spouse really wanted it?
    ☐ Yes   ☐ Sometimes   ☐ Never

Do you expect your partner to prepare your breakfast?
    ☐ Yes   ☐ Sometimes   ☐ No

Do you eat breakfast?
    ☐ Yes   ☐ Sometimes   ☐ No

Do you eat a cooked breakfast?
    ☐ Yes   ☐ Sometimes   ☐ No

When you have children, who will prepare breakfast?
    ☐ Myself   ☐ We will share   ☐ My partner

If your partner, who normally prepares breakfast or dinner, had a change in their work hours that made it inconvenient for them to do so, would you be willing to step in?
    ☐ Yes   ☐ Sometimes   ☐ No

How do you feel about watching television during dinner?
    ☐ It should never happen; dinnertime is family time.
    ☐ It is OK occasionally.
    ☐ It is fine; that is how I grew up.

✷ ✷ ✷

Sleep

What type of mattress do you prefer?
- ☐ Spring coil (☐ very firm ☐ firm ☐ plush) ☐ Pillow top
- ☐ Memory foam   ☐ Sleep number/adjustable

Would you be bothered if your partner insisted on a mattress type that wasn't your first choice?
- ☐ Yes   ☐ Not sure   ☐ No

Which of the following describes your preferred sleep pattern?
- ☐ Go to bed early, get up early
- ☐ Go to bed late, get up late
- ☐ Go to bed anytime, get up anytime

Would you be bothered if your partner had an opposite sleep pattern from you?
- ☐ Yes   ☐ Not sure   ☐ No

Which of the following sleep issues apply to you?

- ☐ Snoring   ☐ Sleep apnea   ☐ Sleep talking
- ☐ Insomnia   ☐ Sleep paralysis   ☐ Need for earplugs or blindfolds

SLEEP

☐ Frequent movements ☐ Need for sleeping pills ☐ Frequent nightmares

Would you be bothered if your partner had any of the sleep issues mentioned above?
　　☐ Yes　　　☐ Not sure　　　☐ No

If so, which ones? _____ _____ _____

What would you do if your partner was significantly affected by one or more of the sleep issues mentioned above?
　　☐ Insist that my partner sleep in another room
　　☐ Move to another room to sleep
　　☐ Insist that my partner receive professional therapy
　　☐ Put up with it/them so we can sleep together

What size mattress do you prefer?
　　☐ Full　　　☐ Queen　　　☐ King

With respect to light, what type of sleep environment do you prefer?
　　☐ As dark as possible at night and in the morning
　　☐ Slight light at night, but no sunlight in morning
　　☐ Slight light at night, with sunlight in morning
　　☐ Other
　　☐ No preference

Would you be bothered if your partner required an opposite sleep environment from you?
　　☐ Yes　　　☐ Not sure　　　☐ No

With respect to temperature, what type of sleep environment do you prefer?
- ☐ Room cool, sleep under covers
- ☐ Room comfortable, sleep with little or no covers
- ☐ No preference

How long do you usually sleep on a work or school night?
- ☐ Greater than 8 hours
- ☐ 6.5 to 8 hours
- ☐ Less than 6.5 hours

How long do you usually sleep on the weekends?
- ☐ Greater than 8 hours
- ☐ 6.5 to 8 hours
- ☐ Less than 6.5 hours

If you wanted to sleep late into the morning, would it bother you if your partner was involved in an activity that was producing noise like playing loud music or running the vacuum cleaner?
- ☐ Yes   ☐ Not sure   ☐ No

✯ ✯ ✯

Past Relationships

How would you react if your partner told you he or she wanted to have lunch with an ex-relationship?
- ☐ I trust you, go right ahead.
- ☐ I don't know why you would want to do that, but I won't stop you.
- ☐ I really would rather you not do that.
- ☐ If you do that, our relationship is over.

Do you want to keep in contact with any ex-relationships?
- ☐ Yes ☐ Not sure ☐ No

If a person from an old relationship contacted you just to talk, how would you react?
- ☐ Stay in contact and not tell your partner, since you are not doing anything wrong
- ☐ Talk to your partner about it
- ☐ Tell your ex that you are currently in a relationship, and it would not be right to be in contact

Would you want to keep cards, letters, and photos from past relationships?
- ☐ Yes, everything
- ☐ I would like to keep some things like prom photos.
- ☐ If they bothered my partner, I would destroy everything.
- ☐ I don't have anything.

If your partner told you they wanted to keep all the cards, letters, and photos from past relationships, how would you react?
- ☐ No problem; it is the past.
- ☐ It bothers me a little, but I won't make an issue of it.
- ☐ I would want them to keep some pictures and throw away all cards and letters.
- ☐ They must throw everything away, and that is non-negotiable.

How would you react if your partner compared you to an ex-relationship?
- ☐ No big deal; it is only natural to do this.
- ☐ I'm a little upset, but I won't make an issue of it.
- ☐ I'll compare them to one of my ex-relationships.
- ☐ I'll get upset and request that it never happen again.

How would you react if your partner told you that they still "loved" a former partner but were not "in love" with them?
- ☐ I understand how they feel, and I may even feel the same way myself.
- ☐ I don't really understand it, but I know you are really in love with me now, so it is not a major issue.
- ☐ I am very bothered, and we need to have a serious talk about this.
- ☐ This will end or come close to ending our relationship.

How would you react if your partner's family compared you to a past relationship of your partner?
- ☐ I obviously don't like it, but I consider it part of the territory of being in a relationship.
- ☐ I will confront them for being rude.
- ☐ I will insist that my partner speak to their family and assure me that it won't happen again.

PAST RELATIONSHIPS

Do you believe that you can really be "just friends" with a past relationship?
    ☐ Yes   ☐ Not sure   ☐ No

How would you feel if your partner told you that he or she was thinking about hiring someone from a past relationship?
- ☐ I would be OK with it, as long as it was a good business decision.
- ☐ It would bother me, but I wouldn't stop it.
- ☐ I would not allow it.

✭ ✭ ✭

Pets

What type of pet/pets would you like to have?
- ☐ Dog ☐ Cat ☐ Bird
- ☐ Pond fish ☐ Horse ☐ Freshwater aquarium fish
- ☐ Saltwater aquarium fish ☐ Other_____

Would you ever have a pet that you would keep outside all the time?
☐ Yes ☐ Not sure ☐ No

Is there a type of pet that you are absolutely opposed to?
_____

Is there a particular type of animal you would want?
_____

If you wanted a particular pet and your partner didn't, would you be willing to take care of that pet 100% of the time?
☐ Yes ☐ Not sure ☐ No

Would you choose the type of house that you buy based on pet needs?
☐ Yes ☐ Not sure ☐ No

If you do not want a pet, what is the primary reason?
- ☐ They are too expensive to keep

- ☐ They limit your ability to travel
- ☐ They mess up the house
- ☐ I am allergic
- ☐ I just don't like animals
- ☐ We do not have time to care for them

If your partner absolutely wanted a certain pet and you didn't, how would you react?
- ☐ I allow the pet because I want to make my partner happy.
- ☐ I allow the pet, and I also expect to get or do something that my partner doesn't approve of.
- ☐ I allow the pet, but I am not happy.
- ☐ It is either me or the pet.

Would you ever allow a pet to sleep in your bed?
☐ Yes   ☐ Not sure   ☐ No

If you wanted a dog or a cat, would you pay extra money for a pure breed?
☐ Yes   ☐ Not sure   ☐ No

If circumstances rendered you unable to adequately care for your pet, what would you do?
- ☐ That would never happen.
- ☐ Find a friend or relative to care for it.
- ☐ Place it for adoption at a rescue.
- ☐ Euthanize it if there were no other options.

If you were not fond of a pet that your partner owned prior to your relationship, would you allow the pet to live with you?
☐ Yes   ☐ Not sure   ☐ No

If your pet became ill and required a $2,000 operation to become well, what would you do?
- ☐ Find the money and have the operation performed.
- ☐ Talk to my partner before deciding what to do.
- ☐ Strongly consider putting the animal to sleep.

Would you be interested in entering your pet in a pet show?
☐ Yes ☐ Not sure ☐ No

Would you tolerate some mess in your house to allow your pet unlimited access to the outside through a pet door?
☐ Yes ☐ Not sure ☐ No

Would you adopt a pet with a prior behavior issue?
☐ Yes ☐ Not sure ☐ No

✶ ✶ ✶

Vacations

Would you ever consider a separate vacation from your partner?
    ☐ Yes   ☐ Not sure   ☐ No

What type of vacation do you prefer?
- ☐ Relax at a beach or resort
- ☐ Cruise
- ☐ Escorted bus tour of cities/countries
- ☐ Active: hiking, biking, etc.
- ☐ Casino, shows
- ☐ Disney/theme park
- ☐ Explore other cities/countries
- ☐ Exotic, once in a lifetime
- ☐ A different type every time
- ☐ No preference
- ☐ Other_____

Are you interested in visiting the following countries, continents, and regions?

Europe	☐ Definitely	☐ Maybe	☐ Never
Asia	☐ Definitely	☐ Maybe	☐ Never
Africa/Safari	☐ Definitely	☐ Maybe	☐ Never
Australia	☐ Definitely	☐ Maybe	☐ Never

North Africa/ Middle East	☐ Definitely	☐ Maybe	☐ Never
Alaska/Canada	☐ Definitely	☐ Maybe	☐ Never
Mexico/ Caribbean	☐ Definitely	☐ Maybe	☐ Never
Pacific Islands	☐ Definitely	☐ Maybe	☐ Never
South America	☐ Definitely	☐ Maybe	☐ Never

Do you need to go on vacation every year?
    ☐ Yes   ☐ Not sure   ☐ No

How do you feel about vacations and children?
- ☐ We should enjoy some major vacations now before we have children.
- ☐ We should try to take some major vacations with the children.
- ☐ We should postpone major vacations until the children are grown and we are financially stable.

How do you feel about taking vacations with your in-laws?
- ☐ In-laws would be welcome most of the time—they make good babysitters.
- ☐ I would tolerate a few vacations with my in-laws.
- ☐ I will never go on vacation with my in-laws.

If your partner wanted to go on a type of vacation that you did not like, how would you react?
- ☐ Let's go and have a good time. After all, we will be on vacation.
- ☐ I'll go, but I expect my partner to compromise on something that he or she doesn't want to do.

VACATIONS

- ☐ I'll try to talk my partner out of going; if I don't think I'll have a good time, he or she probably won't either.
- ☐ I refuse to go.

How do you feel about going on vacation with friends?
- ☐ It is fun most of the time.
- ☐ It would be fun to do occasionally
- ☐ Those situations always lead to stress and loss of friendships.

Would you consider placing the cost of a major vacation solely on a credit card and pay for it over time?
- ☐ Yes; most people do.
- ☐ Maybe once or twice if we didn't have all the money at the time.
- ☐ Never; that practice can only get us into trouble later.

How much money should we spend on vacations every year?
- ☐ Less than $1,000
- ☐ $1,000 to $5,000
- ☐ $5,000 to $10,000
- ☐ Greater than $10,000

What is your attitude toward flying on large airplanes?
- ☐ I am fine with flying on them.
- ☐ I will travel on them, but I try to avoid them.
- ☐ I will not fly on one.

What is your attitude toward flying on small commuter airplanes?
- ☐ I am fine with flying on them.
- ☐ I will travel on them, but I try to avoid them.
- ☐ I will not go on one.

What is your attitude toward traveling on large cruise ships?
- ☐ I am fine with traveling on them.
- ☐ I am somewhat uncomfortable on them, but I will go on one if my partner really wants to.
- ☐ I will not go on one.

Would you ever consider buying a boat?
- ☐ Yes   ☐ Not sure   ☐ No

Would you purchase a vacation home for your major vacations?
- ☐ Yes   ☐ Not sure   ☐ No

Would you invest in a 'time share" for your major vacations?
- ☐ Yes   ☐ Not sure   ☐ No

✭ ✭ ✭

Holidays

What do you like to do on New Year's Eve?
  ☐ Go to a party ☐ It doesn't matter ☐ Stay at home

How would you like to spend the Thanksgiving holiday as a couple?
  ☐ I want to always have dinner at my home.
  ☐ I want to always have dinner at my parents' home.
  ☐ I want to alternate having dinner at my parents' home, my partner's parents' home, and maybe sometimes at my home.
  ☐ It is all too much trouble; I would like to go to a restaurant most of the time.

How do you feel about decorating your home for holidays?
  ☐ I enjoy it very much, and it is very important to me for all holidays.
  ☐ I like to do it for major holidays only.
  ☐ It doesn't matter to me—my partner can do it as long as it doesn't cost too much.
  ☐ It is a waste of time and money.

How would you like to spend the major religious holidays?
- ☐ At our home with the children
- ☐ At my parent's home
- ☐ Different places, depending on the status of children
- ☐ It doesn't matter to me

How do you feel about going on vacation during the major holidays?
- ☐ I will do it anytime my partner wants to.
- ☐ I would do it occasionally.
- ☐ I am against it. Holidays are not for vacations.

How do you feel about sending out greeting cards during holidays?
- ☐ I enjoy doing it.
- ☐ I like it, as long as my partner does most of it.
- ☐ It is a waste of time and money.

✫ ✫ ✫

Hobbies

List your three favorite hobbies:

_____   _____   _____

How much money per year would you spend on hobbies?
- ☐ Less than $500 ☐ $500 to $2,000 ☐ Greater than $2,000

How do you feel about the equity of both partners in the relationship spending money on hobbies?
- ☐ My partner should spend as much as he or she requires to make him or her happy.
- ☐ We don't have to spend precisely the same amount, but we should set a household budget for hobbies.
- ☐ Both of us should establish a budget for spending the same amount of money on hobbies.
- ☐ At this stage in our life, there are better things to spend money on.

How do you feel about getting your partner interested in your hobbies?
- ☐ I welcome that.
- ☐ Some occasional involvement would be nice.
- ☐ Hobbies are meant to be enjoyed with people other than my partner.

How would you react if your partner wanted to spend a large amount of money on a hobby-related item that you are not interested in (e.g., $5,000 for a telescope) and pay for the purchase with a credit card?
- ☐ That's OK.
- ☐ Sure, and I want to charge the same amount on something for myself.
- ☐ I allow it only if they save for it, and I would not allow it to be charged.
- ☐ I do not allow it; that is too much money to charge.

How would you feel if your partner decided to participate in a dangerous hobby such as mountain climbing?
- ☐ I'm fine with whatever makes them happy.
- ☐ I will try to discourage it, but ultimately it is their decision.
- ☐ It could end our relationship.

✫ ✫ ✫

Religion

Which best describes your religious beliefs and behavior?
- ☐ I believe in God, am part of an organized religion, and attend services regularly.
- ☐ I believe in God, am part of an organized religion, and attend services occasionally.
- ☐ I believe in God, am supposed to be part of an organized religion, but rarely attend services.
- ☐ I am agnostic.
- ☐ I am spiritual but do not believe in organized religion.
- ☐ I am an atheist.

How important is it that your partner have the same attitude toward religion as you do?
☐ Very important ☐ Somewhat important ☐ Not important

How important is it that your partner belong to the same organized religion as you do?
☐ Very important ☐ Somewhat important ☐ Not important

How important is it that your children are raised in your religion?
☐ Very important ☐ Somewhat important ☐ Not important

Would you ever consider converting to your partner's religion?
☐ Yes ☐ Not sure ☐ No ☐ Not applicable

Would it bother you if you were asked to raise your children in your partner's religion?
☐ Yes   ☐ Not sure   ☐ No   ☐ Not applicable

How much money do you expect to contribute to your organized religion each year?
☐ None   ☐ Less than $500
☐ $500–1,500   ☐ Greater than $1,500

Is it important to you to live in a neighborhood with other families of the same religion as you?
☐ Yes   ☐ Not sure   ☐ No

Do you believe in trying to convert others to the same religion as you?
☐ Yes   ☐ Not sure   ☐ No

Would you ever want to hold religious meetings in your home?
☐ Yes   ☐ Not sure   ☐ No

Would you ever want to go on a religious vacation?
☐ Yes   ☐ Not sure   ☐ No

How do you feel about having religious pictures, statues, or artifacts in your home?
☐ They are important to me; I want some in my home.
☐ I would consider having a few if my partner wanted them.
☐ I do not want any.

Do you believe in the power of prayer?
☐ Yes   ☐ Not sure   ☐ No

RELIGION

Do you believe in miracles?
  ☐ Yes   ☐ Not sure   ☐ No

Which of the following theories regarding the origin of life do you believe?
  ☐ Creationism
  ☐ Intelligent design
  ☐ Evolution

How do you feel about religious greeting cards?
  ☐ They are important to me.
  ☐ It doesn't matter to me.
  ☐ I don't like them.

✶ ✶ ✶

School/Education

Do you plan on furthering your education at some time in the future?
☐ Yes ☐ Not sure ☐ No

Do you expect your partner to further his or her education so that he or she can get a better job?
☐ Yes ☐ Not sure ☐ No

Are you willing to make short-term sacrifices like working two jobs or living with parents so that your partner can go to school to have a better job in the future?
☐ Yes ☐ Not sure ☐ No

Are you willing to live in a smaller house so your children could be in a better school system?
☐ Yes ☐ Not sure ☐ No

Are you be willing to make severe financial and lifestyle sacrifices so that your children can go to private schools?
☐ Yes ☐ Not sure ☐ No

Do you expect your parents (or your partner's parents) to help with your children's college education?
☐ Yes ☐ Not sure ☐ No ☐ Not applicable

Which of the following best describes your attitude toward establishing a college fund for your children?
☐ It is a major priority.

SCHOOL/EDUCATION

☐ I expect to have some money set aside to pay for part of their education.
☐ I had to pay for my own education, and I expect my children to do the same.

Which of the following best describes your attitude toward influencing your child toward a particular career?
☐ I expect them to take over the family business.
☐ I would like them to pursue the same career path that I did.
☐ Whatever they do is fine, as long as they choose a career that allows them to make an adequate salary.
☐ Their career choice is entirely up to them.

Would you ever consider withholding college fund money if your child wanted to pursue an area of study that you did not agree with?
☐ Yes   ☐ Not sure   ☐ No

Will you encourage your child to go out of state to college for more life experience?
☐ Yes   ☐ Not sure   ☐ No

Will you encourage your child to attend a local college to remain close to you or to save on living expenses?
☐ Yes   ☐ Not sure   ☐ No

Do you think the theory of evolution should be taught to your children?
☐ Yes   ☐ Not sure   ☐ No

✫ ✫ ✫

Health

What is your general attitude toward health?
- ☐ It is the most important thing in life, and I will always try to exercise, eat right, sleep right, and make medical appointments for preventive health.
- ☐ It is important, and I try to incorporate proper diet, exercise, and prevention into my busy routine.
- ☐ There needs to be a balance between living healthy and enjoying life.
- ☐ You only live once, so enjoy your time to the fullest.

If your partner's attitude toward health is very different than yours, what will you do?
- ☐ There is not much you can do—it is their life.
- ☐ I'll try to persuade them to change by setting an example.
- ☐ I'll insist on certain changes.

Do you believe in the medical benefit of vaccination?
- ☐ Yes ☐ Not sure ☐ No

Do you believe in living wills, "do not resuscitate" orders, and hospice care?
- ☐ Yes, there is no need for unnecessary suffering at the end of life.
- ☐ Only in extreme circumstances.
- ☐ No, God should decide when the end of life comes.

HEALTH

Will you make it a point to encourage your children to live a healthier lifestyle than you do?
 ☐ Yes   ☐ Not sure   ☐ No   ☐ Not applicable

Do you believe in the health benefits of high doses of vitamins?
 ☐ Yes   ☐ Not sure   ☐ No

Do you believe in alternative medicine approaches to serious diseases like cancer?
 ☐ Yes   ☐ Not sure   ☐ No

Do you believe in preventive medicine?
 ☐ Yes   ☐ Not sure   ☐ No

Would you ever not take medicine prescribed to you by a medical doctor because it was too expensive?
 ☐ Yes   ☐ Not sure   ☐ No

Would you ever not have health insurance because it is too expensive?
 ☐ Yes   ☐ Not sure   ☐ No

☆ ☆ ☆

Sports

What sports do you like to play?

_____   _____   _____

What sports do you like to watch?

_____   _____   _____

Is it important that your partner is interested in the same sports as you?
 ☐ Yes   ☐ Not sure   ☐ No

How much money do you spend a year on expenses related to sports participation?
 ☐ Less than $500   ☐ $500–1,500   ☐ Greater than $1,500

How much money do you spend a year on expenses related to spectator sports (not counting those related to your children)?
 ☐ Less than $500   ☐ $500–1,500   ☐ Greater than $1,500

Would you ever place your desire to participate in or to watch certain sports ahead of family matters/events?
 ☐ Yes   ☐ Not sure   ☐ No

Would you ever insist that your children play a certain sport if they were not interested in playing?
 ☐ Yes   ☐ Not sure   ☐ No

SPORTS

Would you spend $500 or more for sports memorabilia?
☐ Yes ☐ Not sure ☐ No

✯ ✯ ✯

House/Home Life

Where do you prefer to live?
- ☐ City   ☐ Suburb   ☐ Rural   ☐ Doesn't matter

Which would you prefer?
- ☐ Larger house, less spending money
- ☐ Smaller house, more spending money
- ☐ Not sure

Do you prefer?
- ☐ Ranch home
- ☐ Condominium
- ☐ Two-story home
- ☐ Not sure

Which of the following must you have in your house?
- ☐ Open floor plan
- ☐ Nice views
- ☐ Two stories
- ☐ Associated with good school system
- ☐ Large kitchen
- ☐ Large yard
- ☐ Pool
- ☐ Ranch style
- ☐ More than two bathrooms
- ☐ Four bedrooms
- ☐ Large walk-in closet
- ☐ Close to public transportation
- ☐ Close to place of employment
- ☐ Close to family
- ☐ Finished basement
- ☐ In-law suite
- ☐ Secluded location
- ☐ Whirlpool tub in bathroom

What is your attitude toward a home mortgage?
- ☐ Large down payment, pay off as fast as possible
- ☐ Normal down payment, pay off in thirty years

HOUSE/HOME LIFE

- ☐ Normal down payment, pay off in fifteen years
- ☐ Smallest down payment, refinance to extend payoff as long as possible

Which of the following best describes your attitude toward your first home?
- ☐ Rent until we can afford our dream home
- ☐ Buy a small starter home or condominium first, then buy a better home in the future
- ☐ Rent, buy a starter home, and then buy better homes if able
- ☐ Always live in a condominium

Who will make the majority of the decisions regarding the interior decorating?
- ☐ I will
- ☐ Both of us will discuss and compromise
- ☐ My partner will
- ☐ I would like to hire a decorator

Whom do you envision cleaning the inside of the home?
- ☐ Me
- ☐ Both of us
- ☐ My partner
- ☐ Neither of us: I want to hire a cleaning service or maid

Whom do you envision taking care of the landscaping/cutting the grass?
- ☐ Me
- ☐ Both of us
- ☐ My partner
- ☐ Neither of us: I want to hire a contractor

Whom do you envision doing snow removal at your home?
- ☐ Me
- ☐ Both of us
- ☐ My partner
- ☐ Neither of us: I want to hire a contractor

Which of the following best describes your attitude toward the ideal organization of the inside of the home?
- ☐ Everything should have its place; it should look like a museum.
- ☐ It should be neat and organized most of the time.
- ☐ It is impossible to keep it neat, so why bother?

Who will do your laundry?
- ☐ I will
- ☐ Sometimes me, sometimes my partner
- ☐ My partner

Would you consider having a gun in your home for security?
- ☐ Yes   ☐ Not sure   ☐ No

Which of the following must you have at your home?
- ☐ Exercise equipment
- ☐ Sit-down bar
- ☐ Kids' play room
- ☐ Vegetable garden
- ☐ Pool table
- ☐ Home theater
- ☐ Hot tub
- ☐ Home office
- ☐ Pond
- ☐ Wine cellar

What color kitchen cabinets do you prefer?
- ☐ Light wood
- ☐ Other
- ☐ Dark wood
- ☐ No preference

HOUSE/HOME LIFE

What type of home decorating do you prefer?
☐ Traditional ☐ Eclectic ☐ Contemporary ☐ other

Do you like to play loud music at home?
☐ Yes   ☐ Sometimes   ☐ No

Do you have trouble throwing things away?
☐ Yes   ☐ Sometimes   ☐ No

✭ ✭ ✭

Marriage Ceremony

Do you want a formal marriage ceremony?
    ☐ Yes   ☐ Not sure   ☐ No   ☐ Not applicable

How much do you want to spend on a marriage ceremony/reception?
    ☐ Less than $10,00   ☐ $10,000–30,000   ☐ Greater than $30,000

How do you expect to pay for a marriage ceremony/reception?
- ☐ The bride's parents will pay.
- ☐ The parents of both partners will pay.
- ☐ Our parents will pay and we will also contribute.
- ☐ We will pay.

Which is the most important with regards to money at the beginning of a marriage?
- ☐ Spend money on the ceremony/reception
- ☐ Spend money on the rings
- ☐ Spend money on the honeymoon
- ☐ Save money for the future

Do you want a traditional wedding reception with the usual expenses of photographer, cake, wedding dress, food/drink, reception hall, and band?
    ☐ Yes   ☐ Not sure   ☐ No

MARRIAGE CEREMONY

Would you ever consider eloping?
☐ Yes ☐ Not sure ☐ No

What are the elements of your ideal wedding reception?

Location _____

Number of guests _____

Food	☐ Sit-down dinner	☐ Buffet	☐ Light hors d'oeuvres only
Drink	☐ Open bar	☐ Cash bar	☐ No alcoholic beverages
Dress	☐ Budget	☐ Up to $1,500	☐ Greater than $1,500
Music	☐ Disc jockey	☐ Live band	☐ Other
Images	☐ Professional photographer and videographer	☐ Photographer only	☐ Other

☆ ☆ ☆

Appearance

Would you ever ask your partner to do any of the following?
- ☐ Dye their hair
- ☐ Lose weight
- ☐ Wear a hairpiece
- ☐ Get cosmetic surgery or use Botox.
- ☐ Get dental work
- ☐ Wear more conservative clothes
- ☐ Wear more provocative clothes
- ☐ Wear a different cologne or perfume

How would you react if your partner asked you to do one or more of the above to improve your appearance?
- ☐ I'll do it.
- ☐ I'll consider some things, but I'm a little bothered.
- ☐ You should be happy with me the way that I am.

How would you react if your partner's appearance dramatically changed in a year or two due to overeating and lack of exercise?
- ☐ I love you the way you are.
- ☐ I'll try to get you to change your habits.
- ☐ It could end the relationship.

✭ ✭ ✭

Shopping

Do you enjoy shopping?
☐ Yes ☐ Sometimes ☐ No

Is it important that your partner go shopping with you?
☐ Yes ☐ Sometimes ☐ No

Whom do you envision doing the grocery shopping?
☐ I will ☐ Both of us ☐ My partner

Is there any shopping that you absolutely must be a part of?
☐ Yes ☐ Not sure ☐ No

If so, what?_____

Would it bother you if your partner excessively used coupons?
☐ Yes ☐ Not sure ☐ No

Would it bother if your partner always wanted to find the cheapest price?
☐ Yes ☐ Not sure ☐ No

✫ ✫ ✫

Addictions

Which of the following do you enjoy?
- ☐ Drinking alcohol
- ☐ Taking recreational drugs
- ☐ Surfing the Internet
- ☐ Playing video games
- ☐ Gambling
- ☐ Smoking cigarettes
- ☐ Watching television

How many alcohol drinks a week (one drink is considered a 12 oz. beer, a shot, or a glass of wine) would you tolerate your partner consuming before it would bother you?
- ☐ Any amount would bother me
- ☐ Seven
- ☐ Fourteen
- ☐ Twenty-one
- ☐ He or she can drink any amount as long as they can function at home and at work.

How much time would you tolerate your partner spending on the Internet each day for non-business-related activities before it would bother you? _____ .

How much time would you tolerate your partner spending each day playing video games without you before it would bother you? _____ .

How much money would you allow your partner to lose per year on gambling before it would bother you? _____ .

ADDICTIONS

How much time per week would you tolerate your partner watching television you didn't want to watch before it would bother you? _____ .

If you are a smoker, when do you intend to quit?
- ☐ In the immediate future
- ☐ I tried in the past, and I will try again soon
- ☐ I don't want to quit now

If you are a smoker, do you smoke in the house?
☐ Yes ☐ Sometimes ☐ No

If you enjoy alcohol, is it important that your partner enjoys it with you?
☐ Yes ☐ Sometimes ☐ No

If you found out that your partner had a past problem with addictions but is fine now, would it bother you?
☐ Yes ☐ Not sure ☐ No

✫ ✫ ✫

Intimacy

Do you like to hold hands in public?
☐ Yes ☐ Sometimes ☐ No

Do you like to cuddle while sleeping?
☐ Yes ☐ Sometimes ☐ No

How would you react if you found out your partner went to a gentlemen's club or male stripper club?
☐ It's not a big deal; I know he or she loves me.
☐ I am OK with it as long as it is not on a regular basis.
☐ It bothers me, and I need to talk with my partner about why they do it.
☐ It could end the relationship if it happens again.

How would you react if you found out that your partner was talking to "singles looking to meet other singles" in an Internet chat room?
☐ It's not a big deal—those places are just a joke, and I know he or she loves me.
☐ It bothers me, and I need to know that it won't happen again.
☐ I consider it cheating, and it could end the relationship.

During intimate moments, would you like to see your partner be more expressive of his or her feelings?
☐ Yes ☐ Sometimes ☐ No

INTIMACY

Is there something your partner can do to improve the intimacy between you?
- ☐ Yes   ☐ Not sure   ☐ No

If you answered *Yes* above, explain here. _____
_____

Do you feel that "absence makes the heart grow fonder"?
- ☐ Yes   ☐ Sometimes   ☐ No

How important is "complete truthfulness" to a relationship?
- ☐ Nothing is more important.
- ☐ No one can tell the truth all the time; the occasional white lie is OK.
- ☐ How I treat someone is more important than what I say to them.

How would you react if your partner wanted you both to seek professional help for intimacy issues in the relationship?
- ☐ I would go. It could help our relationship.
- ☐ I would feel awkward, but I would go.
- ☐ I would refuse to go.

✯ ✯ ✯

Politics

How would you describe your political views?
- ☐ Very conservative ☐ Conservative ☐ Middle
- ☐ Liberal ☐ Very liberal ☐ Mixed

Is it important that your partner share the same political views as you?
- ☐ Yes ☐ Not sure ☐ No

Would you ever volunteer to campaign for a political candidate?
- ☐ Yes ☐ Not sure ☐ No

Would you ever join a peaceful protest?
- ☐ Yes ☐ Not sure ☐ No

Would you try to influence your children to have your political views?
- ☐ Yes ☐ Not sure ☐ No

Would you try to influence your partner's voting?
- ☐ Yes ☐ Not sure ☐ No

✯ ✯ ✯

Time

How much time would your partner have to spend in the bathroom in the morning for it to bother you?
_____ .

How would you react if your partner was frequently five to fifteen minutes late for events?
- ☐ It's not a big deal.
- ☐ It bothers me, but there is nothing I can do to change them.
- ☐ It could end the relationship.

What is your philosophy toward time management?
- ☐ I always try to be early.
- ☐ I always try to arrive on time.
- ☐ I am always on "island time." Life is too short to stress out over time.

✫ ✫ ✫

Friends

Do you expect your partner to like most of your friends?
☐ Yes ☐ Not sure ☐ No

Would it bother you if your partner had a good friend who had a criminal past?
☐ Yes ☐ Not sure ☐ No

Would it bother you if your partner had a good friend who had an ongoing addiction?
☐ Yes ☐ Not sure ☐ No

Would it bother you if your partner had a good friend who was an atheist?
☐ Yes ☐ Not sure ☐ No

Would it bother you if your partner had a good friend who was a persistent cheater in relationships?
☐ Yes ☐ Not sure ☐ No

How many times a month would you allow your partner to go out with his or her friends without you before it would bother you?
☐ 0 ☐ 1 ☐ 2-4 ☐ 5 or greater

FRIENDS

Would you allow your partner to go without you to a single's bar or club with single friends?
 ☐ Yes   ☐ Not sure   ☐ No

Would you travel a long distance without your partner to visit friends?
 ☐ Yes   ☐ Not sure   ☐ No

If you noticed your partner staring at an attractive friend of yours, how would you react?
 ☐ It's not a big deal.
 ☐ It would bother me a little, but it is not worth arguing about.
 ☐ It is disrespectful, and must stop.

✯ ✯ ✯

Miscellaneous

Do you believe in ghosts?
    ☐ Yes   ☐ Not sure   ☐ No

Do you believe in energy sources that modern science can't explain?
    ☐ Yes   ☐ Not sure   ☐ No

Do you believe that certain groups of humans are superior to others?
    ☐ Yes   ☐ Not sure   ☐ No

Do you believe what you are told in infomercials?
    ☐ Yes   ☐ Sometimes   ☐ No

Do you believe in luck?
    ☐ Yes   ☐ Not sure   ☐ No

Do you believe that everything happens for a reason?
    ☐ Yes   ☐ Not sure   ☐ No

Do you believe that all occurrences are random events?
    ☐ Yes   ☐ Not sure   ☐ No

D you believe in UFOs?
    ☐ Yes   ☐ Not sure   ☐ No

MISCELLANEOUS

Do you believe in hypnosis as a means of therapy?
☐ Yes   ☐ Not sure   ☐ No

Do you believe in astrology and psychics?
☐ Yes   ☐ Not sure   ☐ No

Do you believe in reincarnation?
☐ Yes   ☐ Not sure   ☐ No

If applicable, will you take the last name of your partner?
☐ Yes
☐ No, I want to keep my name.
☐ I want to hyphenate both names.
☐ Not applicable

Will you ask your partner to take dance lessons?
☐ Yes   ☐ Not sure   ☐ No

✯ ✯ ✯

Printed in Great Britain
by Amazon.co.uk, Ltd.,
Marston Gate.